ARIZONA

ARIZONA

Photographs by
GILL KENNY

—— ❖ ——

Text by
KAREN THURE

SKYLINE
PRESS

Produced by Roger Boulton Publishing Services, Toronto
Designed by Fortunato Aglialoro

© 1984 Oxford University Press (Canadian Branch)
SKYLINE PRESS is a registered imprint of Oxford University Press

ISBN 0-19-540600-1
1 2 3 4 – 7 6 5 4
Printed in Hong Kong by Scanner Art Services, Inc., Toronto

Introduction

Arizona jumps out at you like a 3-D movie, immense, film-lab colorful, too scenic to be real. You drive home on a road that winds above a twinkly urban valley, lying lazy and radiant in the sunset's peachy glow; you stop for gas at a station framed by slender palm trees, swaying in gentle welcome to the orange balloon of the moon; down the road, a wind-sculptured sandstone monolith towers darkly above the garish arches of a fast-food restaurant. The dramatic scenery is everywhere; much of it dear and familiar; crinkly purple mountains and prongy giant cacti are straight from the Westerns you watched as a kid. Somewhere in the back of your mind, you wonder when you'll have to shuffle out of the theater and face up to the humdrum realities of homework and dirty snow.

Film analogies are often drawn by former Arizonans who have had to move away. They say they feel like they've bowed out of a Technicolor spectacular and stepped down into the scratchy frames of a low-budget black-and-white flick. They spend the years of exile aching for a landscape that had once at one time seemed unreal.

If the above sounds extravagant, that's because all writing about Arizona winds up in hyperbole. You can't describe the Grand Canyon with measured, mincing syllables. You can't evoke the Hopi Pueblos in banal, spiritless words.

Travel brochures of the 1950s used to call Arizona 'the Land of Contrasts' and now it seems that every other travel booster has picked up on the phrase, but it's still a useful concept, corny though it be. More than 200 miles of prehistoric irrigation canals snake dryly through the desert around Scottsdale's lush garden resorts. The nation's most ancient continually inhabited town—tiny Hopi Oraibi—perches on a mesa some 100 miles away from one of the most massive and modern coal-fired power-plants in the world. Near downtown Tucson, late-model cars whoosh over a freeway that passes the wilting adobes of an historic Hispanic barrio.

In nature, the paradoxes are even greater. A dam on the Colorado suddenly transforms a rocky canyon into an improbable blue lake. One breath-taking hour of straight-up driving sweeps you from glary brown desert to spicy pine forest. The sky over one of the nation's most rain-parched states crackles with some of the most flamboyant lightning displays in the world.

Flamboyant scenery also seems to attract flamboyant personalities—Arizona's history sparkles with larger-than-life characters. Of those who came before the Spanish we know little, but sometimes a special burial does provide clues to the life of an outstanding human being. One grave in Canyon de Chelly cradled a naturally mummified old man who must have been a highly respected leader and master craftsman. His passage to the next world had been aided by a bow and arrow, a digging stick, a feather blanket, and baskets filled with food, all placed with him in the grave. In addition, he was provided with a spindle, and nearly three miles of fine cotton thread tied into size-sorted bundles. The weaving supplies suggested that the old man himself may have produced his exquisite, lacy shroud.

Cave excavations reveal that mammoth-hunters lived in Arizona from as early as 9,000 BC onwards, but it was from 300 BC to about AD 1400 that the most creative prehistoric societies flourished. In addition to elaborate cotton garments, these people made outstanding baskets and pottery. Their craftsmen were using acid to etch complex designs on seashells 300 years before European armor-makers learned to etch crests on breastplates.

No one knows what caused the relatively sudden disappearance of these advanced prehistoric cultures. Drought, illness, foreign invaders—all may have played a part. When the Navajos and Apaches arrived around AD 1600, they found industrious Hopis,

Pimas and Papagoes, probably descended from an earlier people known to them as the Anasazi, meaning 'the Ancient Ones'.

Today famous adobe fortresses such as Montezuma's Castle and lonely mounds strewn with broken pottery paint Arizona with a romantic patina of the past. If you take the time to notice, you can even find it among the stacked-glass skyscrapers in the smoggy modern downtowns. Take off from Sky Harbor Airport in Phoenix and look down on the pithouses of Snaketown, first civilized in 300 BC. Look west from a top-floor Tucson office, and see a network of streambeds that teemed with Indian farmers around AD 900. To the south, you can make out the serene white towers of San Xavier del Bac Mission, one of the most spectacular and beautiful Spanish missions in America.

The first Spanish explorer to enter Arizona was black—Esteban the Moor, a gigantic, lusty opportunist who decked himself with bells and feathers and declared that he was invincible. He swaggered heartily northward until some practical Zunis disproved his invincibility with a few well-aimed arrows.

Esteban was followed by an Italian friar named Marcos de Niza. His sparkling report to the viceroy, which described the humble Zuni villages as 'larger than Mexico City', has earned him a reputation as one of history's great liars. Friar Marcos embroidered his report with glittering details about daily life in Cibola—the natives wore gigantic emeralds, he asserted, and scooped up their mush with golden spoons.

Accompanied by the imaginative Friar Marcos, Coronado put on his gilded armor and set out to plunder the riches of Cibola. He led a convoy of the most distinguished young gentlemen in the New World, all confident of making fabulous fortunes; but when the survivors stumbled home from Arizona, their armor was dull and dented by rocks hurled from Zuni parapets. No one knows how Coronado kept his men from butchering their friar guide.

Once the dream of fabulous wealth had faded, Spain dumped the job of colonizing Arizona into the hands of the priests. Another larger-than-life figure took over for Coronado—ascetic, energetic Father Eusebio Kino, founder of San Xavier del Bac and one of Arizona's most beloved heroes. He traveled from mission to mis-sion on a spry mustang, he slept under the stars on a pack-saddle pillow, he sincerely tried to improve the lives of the Indians with imported livestock and seeds. Today, Kino's recently discovered skeleton lies in ostentatious display under glass in the plaza of Magdalena, Sonora, Mexico. It is a tribute to his remarkable charisma that even nonbelievers usually view the ochre bones with uncanny reverence.

Super-personalities like Kino glamorize our ideas of life on the Arizona frontier. They make us forget the gruelling daily routine that most resident priests endured. Father Segesser, who labored at an Arizona mission called Guevavi, gives us a glimpse of the demands of a hot summer's day in 1737. After dashing through a horde of duties from sunrise to mid-afternoon, Segesser eats and retires to his room: 'Now comes the siesta, the time when it is customary here for everyone to take his afternoon repose, except the father, who uses this most quiet hour of the day to write or read whatever seems necessary. Birds also sleep during siesta. When they awaken, the turmoil begins again. The cook demands meat for the evening meal . . . the baker wants flour for baking. And finally, after catechism, the father must go, shovel in hand, to the garden and work there until Avé María.'[1]

Two adobe fortresses—Tubac and Tucson—were built to protect overworked priests like Segesser from raiding Apaches. But the aging, corpulent body of Spain's Mexican empire decayed from within. In 1821, rebellious peasants toppled the sagging government and Arizona became a part of independent Mexico. The grandiose missions were abandoned to decay. In the two little forts, soldiers and settlers huddled behind thick mud walls, dreading attack by the Apaches. Then, when the Mexican War and the Gadsden Purchase made Arizona part of the United States, the Cavalry rode in to open up the territory for land-hungry ranchers, miners, politicians and financiers.

We have all thrilled to those dust-kicking Western movies—after a bloody defeat at a boulder-strewn pass, Geronimo flees to his secret stronghold in the mysterious Chiricahua Mountains. Meanwhile, an anonymous party of whooping braves attacks the wagon train—and the men in blue gallop over the ridge at just the right moment. Captain John Bourke, who fought Apaches with General Crook from 1870–86, gives a more accurate picture of military existence during the Indian Wars... 'The humdrum life of any post in Arizona in those days was enough to drive one crazy. The heat in most of them became simply unendurable... There was a story current that... on one day two thermometers had to be strapped together to let the mercury have room to climb'.[2]

Captain Bourke has hit on a subject that's highly sensitive to most Arizonans even today—the bristling summer heat. Actually, just as much as the defeat of the Apaches, it was the invention of the evaporative cooler and later the more efficient airconditioner that opened Arizona to Yankee exploitation. Entering the Union in 1912, the forty-eighth state muddled along as a backward new-comer until after World War II, when the population began to explode. Today it's the second-fastest growing state in America, one of the nation's leaders in high-technology manufacturing.

The burgeoning electronics industry brings back the theme of preposterous contrasts—the town where Wyatt Earp once stalked Frank Stillwell is now a home to IBM. Military jets fly in noisy formation over the towers of San Xavier del Bac Mission, while ski-lifts arch gracefully over the hills on the White Mountain Apache Reservation.

Each year, more and more of the desert slips away under the developers' bulldozers. Vast naked tracts are transformed into irrigated oases, ripe with green lawns, willow trees and miniature lakes. In Fountain Hills outside Phoenix, a high-powered pump shoots a white jet of water 560 feet into the air. In Lake Havasu city on the Nevada border, the painstakingly imported London Bridge spans a manmade channel that buzzes with motorboats.

Such artificial transformations might be disturbing if it were not for the fact that usually only a few miles of driving brings you back to the vastness of unsuburbanized desert. Then the rich, dry smells, the slanting gleam of sunlight, the fragile breeze, the great dusty silence—all these fill you again with a heady sense of Arizona's past. Coronado in his golden armor passed through a scene just like this. The ancient desert endures.

The best way to explore the desert is on foot, preferably on a mild winter morning. Then you can see the uniquely adapted animals, plants, insects, and birds, and here and there, even in the remotest spots, you find little signs of the intrusion of man. You stop to rest near a boulder that's decorated with spiral petroglyphs more than a thousand years old. At the base of the rock lies a rusty 1935 license plate, a reminder of the latest phase of Arizona civilization.

The Indians are still a strong presence here—one-quarter of the state is covered by reservations, and the people who live on these vast windy tracts feel the poignant tug of both worlds. Hopi Helen Sekaquaptewa puts it simply: 'We must choose the good from both ways of living.'[3] Her tribesman, distinguished jeweler Charles Loloma, voices an artistic point of view: 'I believe in our way of life. I think it works for us.... [But] I think any life is an art, any life-style is an art form. Certainly the Anglo way of life can be an art form, too.'[4]

Even in the crowded cities, the rich weave of art and history helps people of widely varied cultures and ethnic backgrounds get along together. You can see the creative power of the past at work during a rodeo parade in Phoenix or Tucson. Marchers and floats portray Spanish conquistadors, Apache warriors, Mexican vaqueros, Anglo gunfighters, and Chinese entrepreneurs. Even the Black Moor Esteban is boldly strutting along. The noise of the crowd burbles with Spanish, English and various Indian languages. The happy cacophony is a reminder of the mix that has made Arizona what it is today.

The noisy crowds are a contrast to the stark and silent beauty of the silhouettes that are pictured on the jacket of this book. Towering as high as fifty feet, surviving as long as two hundred years, the giant saguaro lives only in Arizona and parts of northern Mexico. Like a tall ship tossing on the high seas, the image tingles with romance and excitement, no matter how many times you see it. It's a fitting symbol of the big-screen splendor that sets Arizona apart from all other places on Earth.

Tucson, 1984   KAREN THURE

Note to the Introduction and Captions

1. Theodore E. Treutlein, editor and translator, 'The Relation of Philip Segesser: The Pimas and Other Indians (1737),' *Mid-America* XXXVII (July 1945), p. 163.

2. John G. Bourke, *On The Border with Crook* (New York: Charles Scribner's Sons, 1891), p. 35.

3. Louise Udall, *Me and Mine: The Life Story of Helen Sekaquaptewa as Told to Louise Udall* (Tucson: The University of Arizona Press, 1969), p. 247.

4. Abe Chanin with Mildred Chanin, *This Land, These Voices* (Flagstaff: Northland Press, 1977), p. 15.

5. Refugio Savala, edited by Kathleen M. Sands, *Autobiography of a Yaqui Poet* (Tucson: The University of Arizona Press, 1980), p. 117.

6. Sharlot Hall, edited by C. Gregory Crampton, *Sharlot Hall on the Arizona Strip: The Diary of a Journey Through Northern Arizona in 1911* (Flagstaff: Northland Press, 1975), p. 83.

7. Frank Russell, edited by Bernard Fontana, *The Pima Indians* (Tucson: The University of Arizona Press, 1975), pp. 284 & 309.

8. Tim McCoy with Ronald McCoy, *Tim McCoy Remembers the West* (Garden City, New York: Doubleday and Company, 1977), p. 93.

9. Abe Chanin with Mildred Chanin, *This Land, These Voices*, p. 64.

10. J. Ross Browne, *Adventures in the Apache Country* (Tucson: University of Arizona Press, 1974), p. 31.

11. Rudolfo Gonzales, *I Am Joaquín: Yo Soy Joaquín: An Epic Poem with a Chronology of People and Events in Mexican and Mexican American History* (New York: Bantam Books, 1972), p. 93.

12. Slim Ellison, *More Tales From Slim Ellison* (Tucson: The University of Arizona Press, 1981), p. 9.

13. Ted DeGrazia, *DeGrazia and Padre Kino* (Tucson: DeGrazia Gallery in the Sun, 1979), p. 59.

14. Charlotte J. Frisbie and David P. McAllester, *Navajo Blessingway Singer: The Autobiography of Frank Mitchell, 1881–1967* (Tucson: The University of Arizona Press, 1978), p. 219.

15. Abe Chanin with Mildred Chanin, *This Land, These Voices*, p. 16.

1 Saguaro, *Cereus giganteus*

Beloved symbol of Arizona, the saguaro stands steadfast against constantly
changing cloud-play and light. In the harsh blaze of afternoon or in the soft ashes
of twilight, the thick-skinned plant is a reminder of patience and quiet survival.

2 Organ pipe cactus, *Cereus thurberi*, at Organ Pipe Cactus National Monument along the Mexican Border

The clustered limbs of this relative of the saguaro resemble the pipes of an organ. In the United States, it grows only on the rugged expanse of the Organ Pipe Cactus National Monument. In Mexico, it's much more common. Children there enjoy a sticky candy that's made from the fruits of the organ pipe and the prickly pear.

3 *(right)* Monument Valley, Navajo Reservation

Sand is everywhere on the Navajo Reservation—in the tawny dunes, in the sandstone spires and mesas. And sand lies at the spiritual heart of many of the Navajo healing ceremonies. Chanting religious poetry, the shaman creates an exquisite symbolic picture on sand. Like the ever-changing patterns on the dunes, it lasts only a few brief hours before it's swept away.

4 Whiteriver Sunrise Ceremony, San Carlos Apache Reservation

The Apaches have a rich ceremonial tradition. Elaborately beaded doeskin garments are often worn as part of the ritual. But the most spectacular Apache costumes clothe the mysterious Crown Dancers. Balancing huge, fan-shaped headdresses, their faces dark and secret under featureless black masks, they dance out of the mountains to bestow a blessing. When their wild but regal dance is finished, they vanish into the damps and shadows of the dawn.

5 (right) Sunset in Sedona, Coconino National Forest

In the summer, when afternoon thunderstorms refresh the desert, remnant clouds reflect some of the year's most delicate sunsets. There's something particularly brilliant about the quality of the light, and the fresh-washed air smells of pungent chaparral.

6 *(left)* Santa Rita Mountains reflected in a cattle pond at Sonoita, near the Mexican Border

Around the turn of the century, tattered Yaqui Indians plodded across the Border, political refugees from Mexico. Settling in tiny villages around Tucson and Phoenix, they have shared their unique religious traditions with the people of Arizona. One Yaqui refugee—Refugio Savala—has also given us the gift of his poetry:

> Here I sit in solemn reminiscence,
> Contemplating the evening fall.
> Majestic clouds float in magnificence,
> The setting sun a golden ball,
> Clouds change to roses in the scene,
> Blur the mountains like purple walls.[5]

7 Prickly poppy, *Argemone corymbosa*

This fiesty plant pops up in the most inhospitable places: the dusty shoulder of a freeway, the stony crevice of a ruin. Its lush and delicately crinkled flowers top the prickly leaves like sweet whipped cream. The little plant is humble compared to the kingly saguaro, but it combines the qualities of strength and beauty in much the same way. When most spring wildflowers have wilted under the blast of the summer sun, the prickly poppy endures.

8 *(left)* Roadrunner or chapparal cock, *Geococ-cyx californianus*

Often called 'the desert's clown', the roadrunner is a ground-dwelling member of the cuckoo family. You have to be impressed with his speed and agility—he can race across rough terrain at fifteen miles per hour. He is a meat-eater, and most of his prey consists of rodents, insects, snakes and lizards; but he also relishes the nestlings of the gentle quail, a habit that makes him unpopular with some desert birders.

9 Saguaro *(Cereus giganteus)* in bloom

In springtime, rings of white flowers crown each gesturing limb of Arizona's saguaros. The tough old giants look as if they are holding wedding bouquets. The waxy white Saguaro bloom has been designated the official state flower.

10 Canyon de Chelly National Monument, Navajo Reservation

Natural shelters in the cliffs of Canyon de Chelly have been a refuge to man for nearly 2,000 years. Life was good here—the river nurtured healthy crops and attracted thirsty game. Today the cliff-dwellers' well-preserved ruins make Canyon de Chelly an archeologist's paradise.

11 *(right)* Monument Valley, Navajo Reservation

Winter snows are heavy in Navajo country. In spring they melt into vast expanses of sticky red mud. The mud cracks and dries into hot, glittering dust that grits into your face when the wind blows in a storm. Hissing rain makes the washes run, and the dust turns back into mud again.

12 *(left)* Agaves *(Agave deserti)* and volcanic rocks, near Sedona on Oak Creek

Jumbled black volcanic rocks litter the desert in areas that once swirled with molten lava. They lend an otherworldly look to the agave, a tough succulent plant that normally lives from ten-to-twelve years. At the time of its maturity, a thick, twenty-foot flower stalk springs up from its center, and then the agave in bloom truly appears to belong on another planet.

13 Seneca Falls below Seneca Lake, near the Salt River Canyon on the San Carlos Apache Reservation

Plunging water is a luxury in this dry state—outside the Grand Canyon, only a few year-round waterfalls splash down into rocky gorges. The basic human longing for the life-assuring sound of water is filled by private and public fountains, artificial streams in city parks, irrigation ditches, and rushing arroyos after summer rains.

14 Grand Canyon National Park, looking toward the North Rim and Kaibab Plateau

Sharlot Hall, Arizona's energetic turn-of-the-century journalist, explored the Northern Rim of the Grand Canyon in 1911. She describes a barely accessible wilderness, rife with mountain lions:' . . . The easiest way to reach the Kaibab is from the end of the Grand Canyon railroad, going down the trail to the river at El Tovar; crossing the cable to the northern bank, . . . and climbing up the Bright Angel Trail on the northern side to the camp on the rim, where guides and outfit can be had for lion-hunting excursions. . . . It is an interesting fact that so far more foreigners than Americans have made this trip, and the lions have been sent out alive to parks in England and Germany.'[6]

15 *(right)* Grand Canyon National Park, view from South Rim

Translucent blue ranges suggest a dreamy Shangri-La, and there is indeed a remote little paradise deep in the heart of the Grand Canyon. Cascading waterfalls, tall trees and showy flowers make the Havasupai Reservation a subtropical garden. Like Shangri-La, it can only be reached on muleback or on foot.

16 Scottsdale Ranch Resort Lake, McDowell Mountains in the background

Nurtured by the sudden prosperity of Phoenix, Scottsdale has grown up like a privileged child. From being an awkward hamlet in the 1950s, Scottsdale has become a sophisticated showplace—a riviera of fine restaurants, resorts, boutiques, and costly homes. Water is a status symbol in the desert, and pampered Scottsdale flaunts it like a diamond. More than ten thousand swimming pools, ponds, and artificial lakes accent its velvety lawns.

17 (right) Autumn foliage near Sunrise Lake, Fort Apache Reservation

In Arizona, the seasons are vertical—you find the fall by climbing a mountain. On a crisp evening in the primitive silence of the forest, you wonder what the fall must have meant to prehistoric cliff dwellers here. As the days grew shorter, the tiny rooms of their masonry houses must have grown dark, damp, and cold. In the center of the floor, a smoky fire offered a single spark of warmth.

18 Engelman prickly pear *(Opuntia phaeacantha)* in bloom

The prickly pear's pure yellow blossoms develop into bright violet fruits. Birds and animals devour them like gluttons; people use them to flavor candy and jelly. Desert Indians used to celebrate the ripening of the prickly pear with singing and dancing.

19 *(right)* Bisbee, founded in 1880

You enter the town of Bisbee by driving through a long, dark tunnel in the Mule Mountains. When you come out, you feel as though you've traveled into another time and place. Hilly brick streets, tree-shaded parks, piked iron fences and slate roofs all remind you of Victorian Great Britain. Dr James Douglas, the driving force behind the development of Bisbee's famous Copper Queen Mine, was a loyal British subject of Scots-Canadian descent. He nostalgically created the town in the image of his beloved homeland.

20 Manzanita *(Arctostaphylos)*

In Spanish, *manzanita* means 'little apple,' and this shrub's red berries taste like tart little winesaps. Indians ate them raw or powdered the pulp to make a refreshing drink. Yankee settlers baked them into cobblers and pies that reminded them of desserts in New England.

21 *(right)* Pinaleno Mountains, Coronado National Forest near Safford

When dusk slides over the mountains, daytime colors fade into hazy grays and blues. Two ancient Pima medicine songs describe the dusk and dawn:

> Darkness settles on the summit
> Of the great Stony mountain.
> There circling round it settles
> On the great Stony mountain.

* * *

> The bright dawn appears in the heavens;
> The bright dawn appears in the heavens;
> And the paling Pleiades grow dim,
> The moon is lost in the rising sun.[7]

22 Navajo rug with Navajo jewelry

The magnificent arts of the Navajo reflect their pride in their race. Creativity and patience produce perfection; that's what being a Navajo is all about.

23 Salt River Canyon, Salt River Apache Reservation

A drive through the Salt River Canyon is a rollercoaster ride of twists and turns, of heart-stopping climbs and plunges. If it were near any other major city than Phoenix, the Canyon would be touted as a scenic wonder, but here it tends to be taken for granted.

24 Tawa-Hopi Kachina, spirit of the Sun God

Kachinas are an ancient part of Hopi religious ritual. Both effigies and live Kachina-impersonators embody the spirits of living things. When magnificently clad Kachinas come dancing into a village, your heart begins to pound and your throat grows tight. You know that you are in the presence of a secret and primitive power.

25 Drachman house in Tucson

Water transforms the unruly desert into gentlemanly lawns and gardens. But in Tucson the water table is dropping every year. It's the largest city in the country that relies entirely on groundwater.

26 Gold-and-diamond bola tie

Arizona is the only state with an officially designated neckware. It's the bola tie, an imaginative combination of the cowboy neckerchief-holder and the string bowtie. Invented in the early 1950s, the bola has become a classic form of Southwestern jewelry. Dressy but comfortable, it can be worn on a summer night with the shirt-collar open.

27 *(right)* **Cotton-harvesting at Marana, northwest of Tucson**

Cotton came to Arizona from Mexico. Prehistoric Indians dug a labyrinth of irrigation canals to cultivate this water-thirsty plant. Today Arizona farmers pump more than 550 pounds of water in order to produce a single pound of famous Pima cotton.

28 Arizona trade tokens, collection of John T. Hamilton

When Arizona was a remote Western territory, US coin and currency were often rare. Happy-go-lucky prospectors weighed out gold dust to pay for their whiskey, while thrifty miner's wives charged goods against their husband's paychecks at the company store. Occasionally a merchant or saloon-keeper minted a special metal token that could be used at a discount at his establishment alone. He knew that his customer would return to do more business if he had a pocketful of tokens that were worthless anyplace else.

29 (right) Tim McCoy's pistol and Arrapaho gloves

Unlike the typical movie cowboy, silent star Tim McCoy was a working ranch-hand and an Arrapaho blood brother. Eventually he settled in Arizona and shared his understanding of the Indian mind: 'The old men considered animals, rocks, plants, the very earth itself, living things, brothers possessed of as much life as themselves, and each a gift from the Great Mystery. It is therefore not in the least bit surprising that their initial reaction to the arrival and impact of the white man upon their field of experience was probably not so very different from what ours might be should an extraterrestrial choose to make an exploratory landing within our range of sight.'[8]

30 *(left)* Sunset Crater National Monument, near Flagstaff

Sometime around AD 1050, a volcano spewed sulphury ash over eight hundred square miles of northern Arizona. When the ash cooled and settled, hearty green plants began to perk up through the newly mineralized earth. The volcanic fertilizer sparked an expansion of prehistoric farming cultures that lasted for more than three hundred years.

31 Morenci, northeast of Safford

Copper miners in Morenci transformed the mountains into stepped pyramids. In other towns, they scooped out vast gaping pits or blasted snaking tunnels. If all of the pure copper taken out of Arizona were melted into a solid mass, it would comprise a monument larger than a sixty-story office building.

32 *(left)* Painted Desert, Navajo Reservation

The bleakness of this weathered scene is what most people expect to find in the desert. They are surprised to discover that even in these badlands, delicate flowers and animals flourish. Shaded crevices and dark burrows protect them against the shimmering sheets of heat.

33 Autumn foliage near Carrizo Creek, south of Show Low

Fall pounces suddenly on the White Mountains. Aspens melt into gold overnight, and the sumac bursts into flame. Walking in the woods in a frosty morning, you can sense the elemental urgency of animals preparing for the cold.

34 Santa Catalina Mountains near Tucson, Coronado National Forest

In the mountains, it rains and snows more often than on the desert floor. Chilly winter temperatures preserve the layers of snowfall, and a ski-lift operates during the coldest months. By noon, people usually shed their jackets to ski in sweaters under the warm winter sun.

35 (right) Snow on Gate's Pass, Tucson Mountain Park

Once in a while a winter storm dusts the desert with snow. It usually melts by 10:00 a.m., but not before excited children rush outside to pelt each other with snowballs. In 1974, Tucson had a white Christmas; people still recall the event with awed delight.

36 Near Hannagan Meadow, south of Alpine, Apache National Forest

Some places in the White Mountains look like Alpine meadows, rich with lush grasses, flowers and trout streams. In the winter, cross-country skiers glide along the streambanks and the air snaps with the clean, fresh smell of snow.

37 *(right)* Lake Powell, Glen Canyon Recreation Area

Arizonans love to build dams. The state has some of the oldest and most massive dams in the country. Glen Canyon Dam trapped the Colorado and transformed it into Lake Powell, with almost two thousand miles of twisting shoreline. Water snakes in and out of ninety-six canyons; the surface reflects the colorful shapes of towering spires and buttes.

38 *(left)* Jumping cholla *(Opuntia fulgida)* and desert marigold *(Baileya multiradiata)* at Organ Pipe National Monument

Late March is the prime flowering season for most low-growing desert plants. In late May, when most of the wildflowers have disappeared, the cacti leap into bloom in loud, swaggering colors.

39 Golden poppies *(Eschscholtzia mexicana)* and lupine *(lupinus sparsiflorus)* near Pichaco Peak, between Tucson and Phoenix

It's hard to believe that delicate flowers can spring out of the rough desert soil, but if winter rains come at just the right time, in spring the hillsides shine with golden poppies. People stop their cars to wade through purple-blue lakes of lupine on the median strips of the highways.

40 Abandoned copper mine, Jerome State Historical Park, north of Prescott

Jerome clings to Mingus Mountain like an old gray cat to a window-sill. Its Victorian houses balance precariously on steep stone terraces; the gingerbread-trimmed porch of one hangs out over the tin roof of the one below. For more than fifty years, miners gouged into the mountain's belly to extract almost a billion dollars worth of copper. When the mines payed out, the picturesque town became an art colony.

41 *(right)* Monument Valley, Navajo Reservation

The vast silent grandeur of Navajo country may be one reason for the intimacy and loyalty that characterize Navajo life. In such an empty and awesome landscape, it's reassuring to know that others care for you. The Navajo express the idea of caring with the phrase 'I'll run after them.' It means, 'I will help the people of my clan, no matter what they may ask of me.'

42 Blue Mesa area, Petrified Forest National Park

These forbidding badlands used to be a grassy plain, shaded by conifers and roamed by dinosaurs. An ancient flood suddenly toppled the trees and buried them in soft clay. Aeon by aeon, cell by cell, the trunks and bark turned to stone. The tree-ring patterns remained the same, but now they were made of marble-like silica, dyed by colorful minerals. What time and nature slowly preserved, modern man is helping to destroy. Vigilant rangers are no match for the hordes of visitors who seem determined to carry off the Petrified Forest piece by piece.

43 Tuzigoot National Monument, near Cottonwood, northeast of Prescott

Huge pueblos like Tuzigoot stand silent and forlorn today, but it's easy to imagine boisterous laughter, meaty smells, the persistent beat of a buckskin drum. Life was short and difficult, but there was time for elaborate religious celebrations; and between the chores of grinding and weaving, there was time to look down on the field in the valley and pray to the gods for rain.

44 Newspaper Rock, Petrified Forest National Park

Pecking away with sharp hard stones, prehistoric artists made their marks on rocks all over Arizona. The designs are similar to the ones that are found on rocks throughout the world. Of all the common motifs, the handprint is the most touching. Some early human being used his or her hand to achieve a kind of immortality.

45 Tonto National Monument, near Roosevelt Lake, northeast of Phoenix

Almost everywhere that you find water in Arizona, you will see prehistoric cliff dwellings nearby. The Indians climbed down to the river each morning to tend their neat rows of beans, corn, and squash. At the appearance of raiding nomads, they scurried back up the cliff to defend their homes with rocks and arrows. The strategic advantages of the cliffside locations were evidently worth all the tedious climbing upward with burdens of food and water.

46 *(left)* Casa Grande Ruins National Monument, near Coolidge

Arizona's hero-priest Father Kino discovered these walls in 1694. By then they had been standing for about 350 years. Rising to a height of four stories, the massive structures are a puzzle—were they part of a watchtower, a temple, a multiple dwelling or even an observatory? There is an eerie feeling about these unusual ruins—they are a mysterious monument to the quirky genius of their makers.

47 Ball court at Wupatki National Monument, north of Flagstaff

This court once smelled of athletes' sweat and rang with shrieks and cheers. If the game was anything like the Aztec contest described by the early Spaniards, it was more like a brawl with a rubber ball than an organized sport. At the end of the competition, the winners had the right to snatch the jewelry of the spectators—a custom that must have resulted in a sudden clearing of the stadium.

48 *(left)* Montezuma's Castle National Monument, east of Prescott

This beautifully preserved limestone-and-adobe fortress is a tribute to the architectural skill of the Sinagua Pueblo Indians, who inhabited it from AD 1100–1400. Arizona archeologist Emil Haury describes the feelings that such ruins inspire. 'When you look at the remains of the oldtimers and you see that they did so much with so little, you can only develop a tremendous respect for them, not only as individuals, but for *Homo sapiens* as a fellow who can get along even through great adversity.'[9]

49 White House Ruins, Canyon de Chelly National Monument, Navajo Reservation

White House is one of hundreds of prehistoric masonry dwellings in wind-swept Canyon de Chelly. Many of the houses nestle in rock shelters high above the canyon floor. People reached them by nimbly scaling the cliffs on pecked hand- and toe-holds and log ladders.

50 Second Mesa, Hopi Reservation

Atop an ancient building, high on a crumbling mesa, the Hopi spirit-talker would stand tall in the dawn. In a resonant chant he would relay the needs of his village to the powerful People of the Clouds. Tales of drought and sickness would boom out over the sunrise. If the Cloud People were listening, they would offer strength and help.

51 Meteor Crater, near Winslow

Thousands of years ago, an eighty-foot-wide chunk of metallic rock broke off a star and flashed down through Space. Its velocity made it white-hot and ponderously heavy—when it slammed into the Earth, it smashed a hole three miles in circumference. Today you can still find shards of the meteorite, shiny and metal-heavy, black and mysterious. Prehistoric Indians put pieces of the star-rock into their ceremonial bundles.

52 Chiricahua National Monument, Coronado National Forest

In a state where spectacular natural rock formations are common, the contortions of the Chiricahuas stand out as outrageous. Thousands of years of wind, rain, and ice have wrested the mile-high mountains into a mass of weirdly balanced rocks and twisted spires. Gaping windows and arches pierce the pinkish sculptures with dramatic bits of blue sky. The extravagant effect is all the more startling because the vegetation is gentle—a deep-green mix of sweetly scented junipers, pines, and oaks.

53 *(left)* Red Rock Crossing, near Sedona on Oak Creek

Red cliffs, tall trees and a cold stream make Oak Creek a favorite picnic spot. It's a softly radiant place, a welcome change from the penetrating glare of the nearby desert. Lying under an old oak on the sandy streambank, listening to the songs of warblers and finches, it's hard to imagine that the commercial bustle of Phoenix is only a couple of hours away.

54 *(left)* University of Arizona area, Tucson

Territorial legislatures were notorious for dubious political maneuvering, but the 'Thieving Thirteenth' of 1885 was a scoundrel among scalawags. Distributing booty like a drunken bandit, it gave the insane asylum to Phoenix and the prison to Florence. The booby prize—the university—went to poor powerless Tucson. Today most people feel that Tucson got the best deal after all. Besides providing the city's largest single source of income, the University of Arizona unites the people of Tucson with intellectual pride.

55 Tucson, with the Santa Catalina Mountains in the background

Looking at clean and modern downtown Tucson, it's hard to imagine the shabby hell-hole that traveler J. Ross Browne described in 1864: '. . . a city of mud-boxes, dingy and dilapidated, cracked and baked into a composite of dust and filth; littered about with broken corrals, sheds, bake-ovens, carcasses of dead animals, and broken pottery; barren of verdure, parched, naked and grimly desolate in the glare of a southern sun.'[10] Unlike Phoenix, Tucson has a long history, but much of it doesn't inspire civic pride.

56 Phoenix Art Museum

The manicured, water-splashed luxury of the ninth-largest US city asserts man's triumphant control over the primitive desert. But on a clear day you can make out the rough purple folds of the Superstition Mountains, humped like an old dinosaur along the horizon to the east. Wrapped in Indian legends and tantalizing tales of lost treasure, their craggy bulk reminds you that the untamed desert persists—and it isn't so very far away.

57 Granite Dells on Watson Lake, North of Prescott

The wrinkled granite flanks of the boulders at Watson Dells look like Arizona itself appears when seen from Space—a tortured membrane of lumpy mountains, valleys, and plains, slashed by the thin blue scars of a few great dying rivers. The color is beige, shading to gray—sallow and inhospitable. Peering down from the window of a spaceship, you would never believe that life could exist in Arizona.

58 Tombstone City Hall, erected in 1882

From 1879–86, Tombstone was an important town that many thought would eventually become the state capital. Contrary to newspaper accounts that built up its lawless image, the silver-boom city was one of the most civilized and sophisticated places in the West. In the luxurious private Tombstone Club, mining executives smoked Havana cigars in rich leather chairs set on Oriental rugs. Debutantes whirled at tea dances complete with Japanese lanterns and French champagne. Then water flooded into the mines, drowning the dream of glory. By the early 1890s, Tombstone was almost a ghost town.

59 Wright-Zellmeger home, Tucson, built in 1900

In territorial days, Tucson was an important supply center for outlying ranches, mines, and forts. Its most prosperous citizens were shop-keepers, who shrewdly put their surplus profits into diversified businesses. Many of these early merchants built fine homes near their downtown stores. After sliding into boardinghouse dilapi-dation over the course of nearly a century, these solid old buildings are now being restored to their original bourgeois splendor.

60 Old Pima County Courthouse, Tucson

Reflecting their pride in their city's past, Tucsonans didn't tear down their old courthouse when they built an elaborate new government complex in 1973. The old building's bright tile dome stands out like a precious jewel among the surrounding stark white skyscrapers.

61 *(right)* Grady Gammage Auditorium, Arizona State University, Tempe

Architects love Arizona. Its rugged scenery provides a distinctive setting for their structures. Frank Lloyd Wright, who designed Grady Gammage Auditorium, also built beautiful Taliesin West, an architectural school and firm in Scottsdale. Its sensitive integration of stone buildings into the desert landscape is a model of terseness and grace.

62 Old adobe home in Fort Lowell historical area of Tucson

This old home used to be part of the officers' quarters at an Apache-fighting post called Fort Lowell. Its two-foot-thick mud walls are reminders of Tucson's earliest history. The first non-Indians to settle the town were Spanish—they erected a mud-walled fort called San Agustín del Tucson in 1766. A nearby Indian village called *Chukson*, or 'At the Foot of Black Mountain', gave the fort—and later the city—its strange but melodious name.

63 Ocotillo *(Fouquieria splendens)* in bloom at the O'Nell Hills, near Organ Pipe
National Monument

The stark ocotillo looks like a giant seaweed that someone has rashly transplanted
from the deep. In the spring, it blooms with bright red-orange flowers shaped like
tropical fishes.

64 Continental Financial Center, Scottsdale

Phoenix and its surrounding communities began as agricultural centers, but today their economies are based on manufacturing, tourism and a thriving variety of business activity. From a farm town of 65,400 in 1940, Phoenix has grown into a metropolis that's nudging a million. The sudden growth has produced some problems, such as smog and traffic congestion, but Phoenix and its suburbs still offer one of the most attractive lifestyles in the country.

65 *(right)* Saguaro *(Cereus giganteus)* outside IBM plant in Tucson

The sturdy saguaro is filled with personality. Each giant uses its limbs to strike a different dramatic pose. When you get to know individual saguaros near your home or place of work, it's impossible not to think of them as friends.

66 Saguaro *(Cereus giganteus)* at the Saguaro National Monument, in the Tucson Mountains

The saguaro is a kindly plant, scratchy though it may seem. Its flanks are scarred and pocked with holes made by the creatures that it houses and feeds. In summer, scarlet saguaro fruit is a favorite with birds, animals and people. Filled with tiny black seeds, it tastes like a cross between a raspberry and a watermelon.

67 *(right)* Little Dragoon Mountains and Texas Canyon, south of Benson

Rock is everywhere in Arizona—a harsh and haunting presence. Much of it is laced with minerals like gold, silver, copper, lead, zinc, molybdenum and uranium. From the days of the early Spaniards, men have grown rich by patiently pecking away at Arizona rock.

68 *(left)* Blacksmith shop at Double Adobe near Bisbee

Tiny Double Adobe is nearly abandoned, but a stubborn blacksmith continues to fire up his forge. His shop is a reminder of the leathery determination that carried Arizona settlers through the bloodiest days of Apache raiding. Pete Kitchen's hacienda near the Mexican Border was the best-known civilian outpost against the Apaches. A sentinel stood constant watch on the parapet, and a loaded rifle leaned in every corner. Eventually the Apaches decided that they had lost enough lives to the tough old man's bullets—with silent discretion they began to pass him by.

69 Chiles *(Capsicum annum)* at Tumacacori Mission National Monument

In the fall, strings of ripe chiles bring to Arizona the same vibrant color that maple trees bring to Vermont. The spicy vegetable was cultivated by the Indians of Tumacacori Mission back in the days of Father Kino. Sweet and pungent, vibrant with flavor, the chile provides a savory base for the slowly simmered, richly condimented Mexican dishes that most Arizonans love.

70 *(left)* Hedgehog cactus *(Echinocereus fasciculatus)* in bloom

The colors of most cactus flowers are rich and deep. It's as if these rugged plants have somehow captured the sun's essence, transformed it, and released it through the petals of their blossoms.

71 Chile harvest in Elfrida, near Douglas

Long growing seasons and abundant sunlight have made agriculture a major Arizona industry. Most of it is done on vast mechanized tracts with computerized programs for irrigation, fertilization, and pest control. Smaller, more personal farms still grow flowers, fruits, and vegetables. Mirgrant laborers pick the harvests with callused fingers.

72 Tlaquepaque Shopping Center, Sedona on Oak Creek

Spanish-style architecture is well-loved in Arizona, and that's because it's at home and comfortable in a desert land. Thick walls of pink, white, or tan adobe stolidy repel the pulsing summer heat. Red-tile roofs contrast grandly with purple mountains, while tiny courtyard gardens offer flowers and intimate shade. The Moors and the Spaniards slowly evolved these architectural concepts. Arizona has taken advantage of their centuries of expertise.

73 'Groupo Folklorico' in Tucson

The rich traditions of Hispanic culture are finely woven into Arizona life. Celebrations ring with the energetic, carefree music of Mexico. Hispanic poet Rodolfo Gonzales describes how it is for his people:

Tramping feet
clamouring voices
mariachi strains
fiery tequila explosions
the smell of chile verde and
soft brown eyes of expectation for a better life.[11]

74 Spanish bayonet *(Yucca baccata)* at Sedona near Bell Rock

In spring and early summer, the yucca's creamy blossoms stand like graceful candles waiting to be lit by the sun. Sweetly fragrant, the flowers tell you that the yucca is a member of the lily family.

75 *(right)* San Xavier del Bac Mission, San Xavier Reservation, south of Tucson

Clouds gather over San Xavier on a summer afternoon. If they mature and rupture into a storm, the Mission's sharp white perfection will blur behind gray curtains of rain. When the storm is over, there will be a cool, dripping silence, and the Papago fields will smell ripe and green.

76 Cowboys at a rodeo in Sonoita, southeast of Tucson

Most rodeo contestants confine their riding to the arena, but a few of them still ride the boundaries of their ranges, fixing fences. Oldtimer Slim Ellison recalls a fence-fixing day in the early part of this century: 'This kind of ridin' is play, not work like roundin' up and brandin'; purty nice in purty country. . . . Lots of range feed of different kinds, wildflowers and lots of game and small critters.'[12]

77 Old Tucson movie location, west of Tucson

The life of a movie cowboy is far removed from the dusty, monotonous reality of a real ranch-hand's existence. But the movie cowboy is one of America's greatest contributions to the world's store of folklore. When you walk the board sidewalks of a film-set like Old Tucson, you feel as though you are a part of the legendary Old West, where good triumphs over evil, and the hero is rugged and free.

78 Spanish bayonet *(Yucca baccata)* in the Santa Rita Mountains, southeast of Tucson

The roots of the yucca contain a natural detergent. Desert Indians use it as a sacred shampoo. When a girl reaches puberty, she tells her mother or grandmother, who begins to organize her coming-of-age dance. Tribal customs differ, but almost all of them include hair-washing in a river with rich, flower-fragrant yucca shampoo.

79 *(right)* Sunset over the Eagletail Mountains, west of Phoenix

Popular artist Ted DeGrazia once wrote about wandering alone in the desert at sunset: 'I stood still for a moment, looking in each direction. To the north, to the south, to the east, to the west. I turned very slowly. The light was refracted, as though emanating from the earth itself. It is that moment on the desert which repays for all of its hardships: its burning heat—its dryness—its harshness. All is forgotten when around you the atmosphere is filled with the diffused light of the setting sun. It makes you feel for a moment like the very center of everything.'[13]

80 *(left)* Boot Hill Graveyard in Tombstone

The man in silhoutte bears a striking resemblance to big-time gambler Dick Clark, supposedly buried in Boot Hill. Dick won and lost vast fortunes on the turn of a card in Tombstone saloons. When the town began to shrivel, he rode posh railroad cars all over the country, in search of the big-stakes poker he loved. In the end, tense nights, whiskey, tuberculosis, and morphine brought him down in his late prime. All of the businesses in Tombstone closed on the day of his funeral.

81 Lynx Lake, Prescott National Forest

Animals and birds who sleep through the unwinking heat of the day creep out into the gentle summer moonlight. Hawks and owls swoop up into the sky. Lions and bobcats slink over the mountains. On the muddy shores of the lake, a solitary raccoon waits for a fish to jump for joy.

82 *(left)* Red sandstone cliffs in Sedona on Oak Creek

The colors of Sedona's wind-worn sandstone change with the movement of the sun. At noon the reds look pink and pale compared to the brilliant crimsons that appear later in the day. At sunset the cliffs suddenly blossom like poppies before they wilt into gray.

83 Sunset over the Santa Rita Mountains in Sonoita

The raw and gaudy splendor of the sunset demands the drama of a coyote's song. but the coyote prefers the star-pocked darkness or the cold, pure light of the moon. His eerie howls and yip-yaps pierce the night like primitive prayers. Then, as suddenly as they began, they stop: silence floats back into the desert on soft bat-wings.

84 Monument Valley, Navajo Reservation

The aloof and splendid beauty of the Navajo's wind-sculptured spires suggest the tribe's sacred Blessingway prayers. Shaman Frank Mitchell shares them: 'As for the prayers, you say, "Beauty shall be in front of me, beauty shall be in the back, beauty shall be below me, above me, all around me." On top of that you say about yourself, "I am everlasting, I may have an everlasting life. I may live on, and lead an everlasting life with beauty." You end your prayers that way.'[14]

85 (right) San Xavier del Bac Mission, south of Tucson

Father Kino established San Xavier in 1700, but the present building was completed by his successors in 1797. San Xavier was dear to the heart of Father Kino— for years he tried to get enough help to allow himself to become its resident priest. You can sense his benign and powerful personality when you step into the dusky silence of the big white church today. Humble Father Kino never aspired to the status of a saint, but he gently and fervently earned it.